AMERICAN PRESIDENTS

RONALD REAGAN

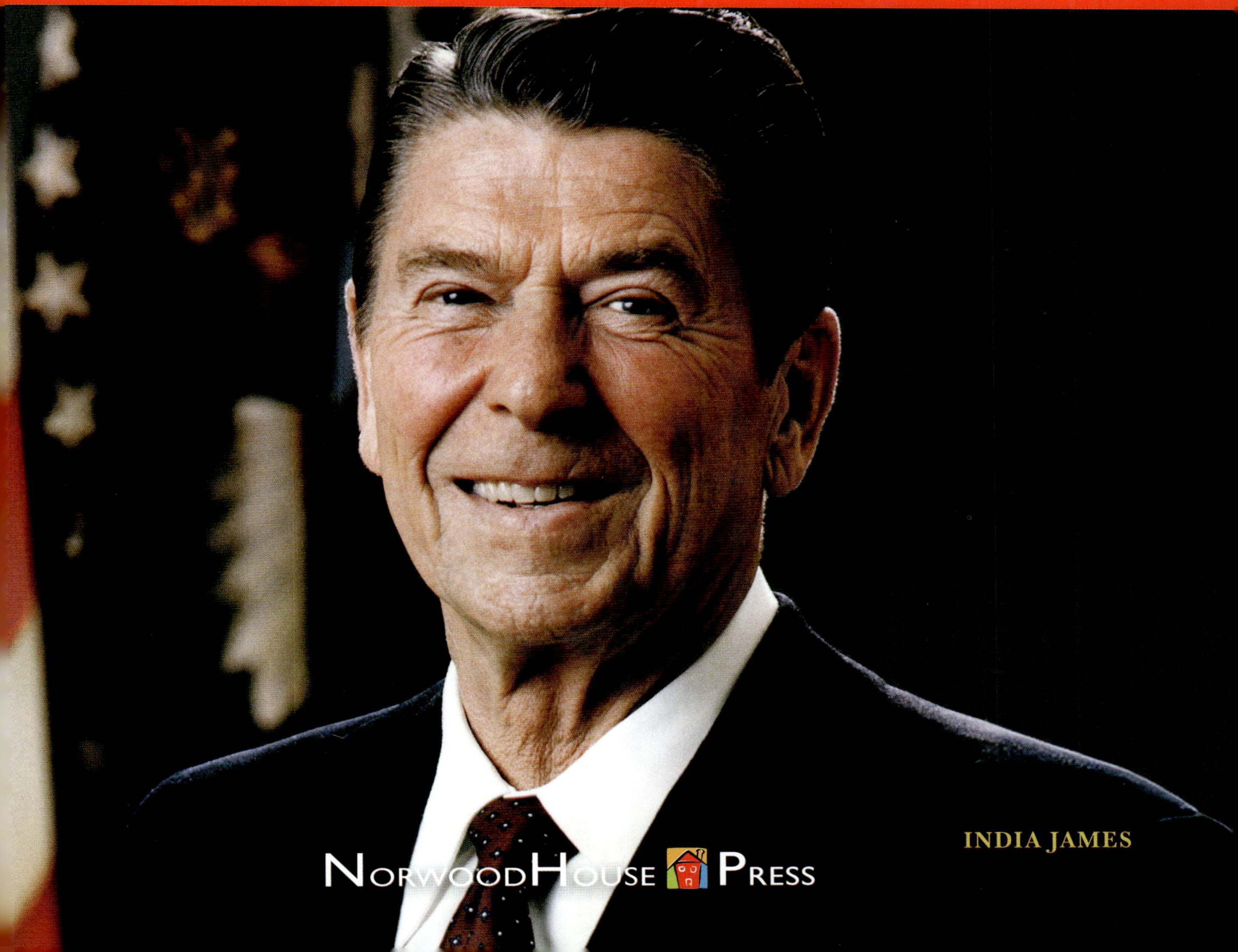

INDIA JAMES

NorwoodHouse Press

Cataloging-in-Publication Data

Names: James, India.
Title: Ronald Reagan / India James.
Description: Buffalo, NY : Norwood House Press, 2027. | Series: American presidents | Includes glossary and index.
Identifiers: ISBN 9781978579934 (pbk.) | ISBN 9781978579941 (library bound) | ISBN 9781978579958 (ebook)
Subjects: LCSH: Reagan, Ronald--Juvenile literature. | Presidents--United States--Biography--Juvenile literature. | Legislators--United States--Biography--Juvenile literature.
Classification: LCC E877. J36 2027 | DDC 973.927092--dc23

Published in 2027 by
Norwood House Press
2544 Clinton Street
Buffalo, NY 14224

Designer: Rhea Magaro
Editor: Kim Thompson

Photo credits: Cover, pp. 1, 5, 7-13, 15-16, 18, 20-21 Wikipedia; p. 5 Library of Congress; p. 19 DacologyPhoto/Shutterstock.com

Printed in the United States of America

CPSIA compliance information: Batch #CSNHP27: For further information contact Norwood House Press at 1-800-237-9932.

TABLE OF CONTENTS

Early Years

Ronald Reagan was born on February 6, 1911, in Tampico, Illinois. He lived with his mother, father, and older brother. The family moved a lot when Ronald was young. Finally, they settled in this house in Dixon, Illinois.

At school, Ronald enjoyed sports, drama, and student government. He played football and was on the swimming team and track team. He acted in many school plays.

Ronald went to Eureka College in Eureka, Illinois. He was elected president of his class.

Building a Career

After college, Ronald worked as a radio announcer. His job was to describe the action during sporting events.

Ronald moved to Los Angeles, California, to act in TV shows and movies. In one film, he played the football player George Gipp. People started calling Ronald "the Gipper." He kept the nickname for the rest of his life.

Ronald married Nancy Davis in 1952. They had two children.

Ronald was good at public speaking. In the 1960s, he became a **politician**. He was elected **governor** of California in 1966 and again in 1970. He represented the Republican Party.

Presidency

Many people liked the way Ronald governed the state of California. They wanted him to run for president. Ronald was elected the 40th president of the United States in 1980.

Two months after Ronald Reagan became president, a man with a gun shot him on a sidewalk in Washington, D.C. Ronald was rushed to the hospital for treatment. He was back at the White House just two weeks later.

THE PRESIDENT OF THE UNITED

YOUR TAXES
AVERAGE FAMILY INCOME - $20,000
1982
1986
THEIR BILL
$

Ronald believed that the government should be as small as possible. It should not control people's lives. He thought that people should keep more of their own money instead of using it to pay taxes. People called his ideas about money **Reaganomics**.

Ronald was president during the **Cold War**. The U.S. and the **Soviet Union** were enemies. Ronald wanted to thaw the war. He gave a famous speech in Germany. It helped convince the Soviet Union to tear down the **Berlin Wall**.

ULSTER STILL SAYS NO

Later Life

Ronald Reagan served two **terms** as president. Soon after his second term, he became sick. He died on June 5, 2004.

Some people called him the Great **Communicator**. He is remembered for his speeches and the power they had to bring peace to the world.

Glossary

Berlin Wall (BER-lin wawl): a wall built in Germany after World War II to separate East Berlin from West Berlin; East Berlin was run by the Soviet Union, and the wall kept people on that side from being free

Cold War (kohld wor): the period from 1945 to 1991 when the U.S. and the Soviet Union were in conflict but did not fight an actual war with weapons

communicator (kuh-MYOO-ni-kay-tur): someone who is effective at speaking and explaining ideas

governor (GUHV-ur-nur): the elected leader of a U.S. state

politician (pah-li-TISH-uhn): a person elected or chosen to hold a government office

Reaganomics (RAY-guh-nah-mics): a set of beliefs about money, including that taxes should be low and that government should not interfere with businesses

Soviet Union (SOH-vee-et YOON-yuhn): a former nation that was divided into several smaller countries in 1991, including Russia and Ukraine

terms (turmz): definite or set periods of time; American presidents are elected to a term that lasts four years

Thinking Questions

1. What activities did Ronald do in school?
2. What were Ronald's jobs before he became a politician?
3. How did Ronald help end the Cold War?
4. Explain Ronald's way of thinking about money.
5. How many times was Ronald elected president?

Index

About the Author

India James writes about science, technology, math, and history for young readers. She loves learning new things while writing books. India lives in Ohio with her family.